DATE DUE

PEOPLE NEED PLANTS!

Mary Dodson Wade

Series Science Consultant:
Mary Poulson, Ph.D.
Associate Professor of Plant Biology
Department of Biological Sciences
Central Washington University
Ellensburg, WA

Series Literacy Consultant:
Allan A. De Fina, Ph.D.
Past President of the New Jersey Reading Association
Chairperson, Department of Literacy Education
New Jersey City University
Jersey City, NJ

CONTENTS

WORDS TO KNOW

broccoli (BRAH kuh lee)—A green food that comes from the flower of a plant.

fibers (FYE burs)—Thin strings in a plant that make them strong or give them shape. Fibers also make the wood in plants strong.

oxygen (AHK sih jen)—A gas in the air that people and animals need to live.

PARTS OF A PLANT

flower

leaf

stem

roots

LIVING WITH PLANTS

Plants are important in our lives. Trees are one kind of plant. Wood comes from trees. People build houses, tables, and chairs from wood. Some people burn wood to heat their homes. People plant trees for shade.

PLANTS WE WEAR

Flax plants have long stems. The long **fibers** in the stem are made into cloth. Cotton plants make fluffy white fibers. Cotton fibers are used to make clothes, such as shirts, pants, and socks.

A farmer checks his cotton plants.

PLANTS WE USE EVERY DAY

Many things we use every day are made from plants. Paper is made from wood fibers. Rope and string can be made from plant fibers. The first chewing gum and rubber balls were made from the juice of a tree.

PLANTS WE EAT

Grains come from the fruit and seeds of grasses. We use lots of grains to make bread, cereal, and cookies. ▶

◀ We also eat roots such as carrots. We eat flowers such as **broccoli**.

Lettuce and spinach ▶
are leaves that we eat.

We eat seeds such
as peanuts and
fruit such as apples.
▼

peanuts

Sugar is made from the stem of a sugarcane
plant.

These birds eat sunflower seeds.

PLANTS FEED
ANIMALS

Animals need plants, too. Most of them eat plants. Squirrels eat nuts. Deer and rabbits like leaves and flowers. Birds eat fruit and seeds. Giraffes eat leaves, and elephants eat grass. Fish eat tiny plants that float in the water.

This pygmy (PIG mee) owl lives in a tree.

ANIMALS USE PLANTS FOR HOMES

Many animals use plants for homes. Owls and bats live in hollow trees. Birds build nests in trees and bushes. Insects live in the bark of trees. Beavers chew down trees to build homes.

Some caterpillars live in trees.

PLANTS THAT HEAL

Many medicines come from plants. Aloes (AL ohs) are plants that make a gel inside their leaves. People put the gel on their skin to help heal a burn.

aloe plant

The gel from aloe leaves can help treat burned skin.

PLANTS AND THE AIR WE BREATHE

Plants help keep us alive. People and animals could not live without the **oxygen** that plants make. They give off oxygen that we need to breathe.

ACTIVITY:

WHAT PLANTS DO YOU EAT?

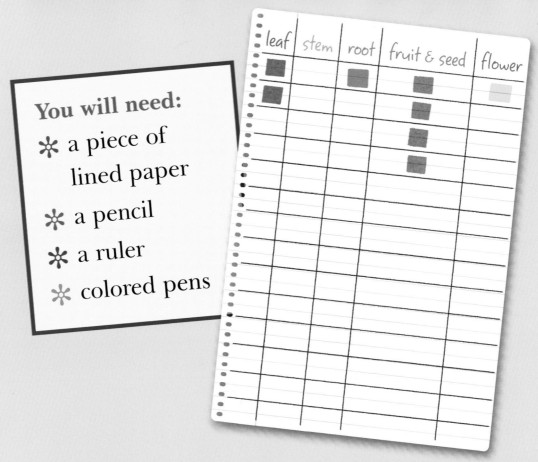

You will need:

- a piece of lined paper
- a pencil
- a ruler
- colored pens

leaf
stem
root
fruit & seed
flower

1. Draw lines from the top of your paper to the bottom to make 5 columns.

2. At the top of each column, write the following words. Use a different color for each word.

LEAF STEM ROOT FRUIT & SEED FLOWER

3. During a meal, look at your food. Color one square for each part of a plant that you eat. (Hints: Some food, like garden salads, may have more than one part of a plant. Other foods, like pizza, have hidden or mashed plant parts.)

4. Look at your chart. Which part of a plant did you eat the most?

5. Use the same chart for three days. Which part of a plant did you eat most during the three days?

LEARN MORE

BOOKS

The Editors of Time For Kids with Brenda Iasevoli. *Plants!* New York: HarperCollins, 2006.

Ganeri, Anita. *From Seed to Apple*. Chicago: Heinemann Library, 2006.

McEvoy, Paul. *Plants as Food*. Philadelphia: Chelsea House Publications, 2003.

Trumbauer, Lisa. *Who Needs Plants?* Chatham, Mass.: Yellow Umbrella Books, 2003.

Rotner, Shirley, and Gary Goss. *Where Does Food Come From?* Minneapolis, Minn.: Millbrook Press, 2006.

WEB SITES

University of Illinois. *Trees Are Terrific.*
<http://www.urbanext.uiuc.edu/trees1/03.html>

University of Illinois. *The Great Plant Escape.*
<http://www.urbanext.uiuc.edu/gpe>

U.S. Department of Agriculture. *Sci4Kids.* **"Plants."**
<http://www.ars.usda.gov/is/kids/plants/plantsintro.htm>

INDEX

Enslow Elementary, an imprint of Enslow Publishers, Inc.
Enslow Elementary® is a registered trademark of
Enslow Publishers, Inc.

Library of Congress Cataloging-in-Publication Data

Wade, Mary Dodson.
    People need plants! / Mary Dodson Wade.
        p. cm. — (I like plants!)
        Summary: "Presents information about how humans and
        animals use plants for housing, food, clothing, and other
        necessities"—Provided by publisher.
    Includes bibliographical references and index.
    ISBN-13: 978-0-7660-3153-1 (library ed.)
    ISBN-10: 0-7660-3153-5 (library ed.)
        1. Human-plant relationships—Juvenile literature.
        2. Plants, Useful—Juvenile literature. I. Title.
    QK46.5.H85W33 2009
    581.6'3—dc22   2007039458

ISBN-13: 978-0-7660-3613-0 (paperback)
ISBN-10: 0-7660-3613-8 (paperback)

Printed in the United States of America

10 9 8 7 6 5 4 3 2 1

Every effort has been made to locate all copyright holders of
material used in this book. If any errors or omissions have occurred,
corrections will be made in future editions of this book.

To Our Readers: We have done our best to make sure all Internet
Addresses in this book were active and appropriate when we went to
press. However, the author and the publisher have no control over
and assume no liability for the material available on those Internet
sites or on other Web sites they may link to. Any comments or
suggestions can be sent by e-mail to comments@enslow.com or to the
address on the back cover.

♻ Enslow Publishers, Inc., is committed to printing our books on
recycled paper. The paper in every book contains 10% to 30% post-
consumer waste (PCW). The cover board on the outside of each book
contains 100% PCW. Our goal is to do our part to help young people
and the environment too!

Note to Parents and Teachers: The *I Like Plants!* series supports the
National Science Education Standards for K–4 science. The Words to
Know section introduces subject-specific vocabulary words, including
pronunciation and definitions. Early readers may need help with
these new words.

Photo Credits: iStockphoto.com: © Adam Tinney, p. 5, © Jani
Bryson, p. 6, © Malcolm Romain, p. 3, © Nancy Louie, p. 4; © 2008
Jupiterimages Corporation, p. 23; © Masterfile, p. 1; Minden
Pictures: © Duncan Usher/Foto Natura, p. 12; naturepl.com: © Rolf
Nussbaumer, p. 14; Photo Researchers, Inc.: Gary Retherford, p. 17,
Kenneth W. Fink, p. 11 (peanuts), Manfred Danegger, p. 13, Nigel
Cattlin, p. 10 (carrots), SPL, p. 16; Punchstock: © Blend Images,
pp. 18–19, © Radius Images, p. 8; Shutterstock, pp. 2, 9, 10 (bread);
Visuals Unlimited: © Bill Banaszewski, p. 10 (wheat), © Clive Nicols/
Gap Photo, p. 11 (spinach), © Inga Spence, p. 7, © Nigel Cattlin,
p. 15, © Paul Debois/Gap Photo, p. 11 (apples), © Wally Eberhart,
p. 10 (broccoli).

Cover Photo: Shutterstock

Enslow Elementary
an imprint of
Enslow Publishers, Inc.
40 Industrial Road
Box 398
Berkeley Heights, NJ 07922
USA
        http://www.enslow.com